Higher Order Thinking Compared to Rote Memorization

Characteristics of the Taxon System
of Information Processing:
(Rote Memorization)

- Requires repetition
- Limited in the amount of information
- Non-transferable
- Most is lost through the decay in a short period of time
- Uses little of the functioning capacity of the brain

Characteristics of the Locale System
of Information Processing:
(Higher Order Thinking)
(Brain-Based Learning
-Problem-Based Learning)

- Processed instantly
- Unlimited in the amount of information it can process
- Transferable to other situations
- Information is retained
- Uses much of the functioning capacity of the brain

Rote memorization is a very inefficient use of the brain!

Adventures in Education Inc. 1997

Book

making connections; teaching of the human Brain

Dont shut down students thinking
— by giving the response quickly

* double entry
X questioning techniques

WRITING IN
SOCIAL STUDIES

GLOBE FEARON EDUCATIONAL PUBLISHER
A Division of Simon & Schuster
Upper Saddle River, New Jersey

Executive Editor: Barbara Levadi

Project Editors: Lynn W. Kloss, Laura Baselice, and Bernice Golden

Writer: Sandra Widener

Production Manager: Penny Gibson

Production Editor: Nicole Cypher

Marketing Managers: Sandra Hutchison and Nancy Surridge

Interior Electronic Design: Richard Puder Design

Illustrators: Accurate Art and Andre V. Malok

Electronic Page Production: Paradigm Design

Cover Design: Mimi Raihl

Acknowledgments

p. 10 (top): courtesy of The Granger Collection, New York; (bottom): courtesy of the New York Convention and Visitors Bureau; **p. 12** (top and bottom): courtesy of United Nations Photo; **p. 66**: courtesy of UPI Photo; **p. 68**: courtesy of U.S. Office of War Information in the National Archives.

Printed in the United States of America.
1 2 3 4 5 6 7 8 9 10 99 98 97 96 95
BF2

ISBN: 0-8359-1897-1

GLOBE FEARON EDUCATIONAL PUBLISHER
A Division of Simon & Schuster
Upper Saddle River, New Jersey

Contents

To the Student   1

Developing Social Studies Skills

Lesson 1   Taking Notes: Reading   2

Lesson 2   Using a Diagram: Main Idea and Supporting Details   4

Lesson 3   Reading and Understanding:
           Main Idea and Supporting Details   6

Lesson 4   Reading and Understanding:
           Analyzing Cause and Effect   8

Lesson 5   Observing: Making Inferences   10

Lesson 6   Observing: Comparing and Contrasting   12

Lesson 7   Answering Essay Questions: Strategies   14

Writing a Report

Lesson 8   Writing a Report: Choosing a Topic   16

Lesson 9   Writing a Report: Taking Notes   18

Lesson 10 Writing a Report: Creating an Outline   20

Lesson 11 Writing a Report: The First Draft   22

Lesson 12 Writing a Report:
           Revising and Footnotes   24

Lesson 13 Writing a Report: Creating an Essay Test   26

Developing Listening and Speaking Skills

Lesson 14 Taking Notes: Listening   28

Lesson 15 Writing an Oral History: Interviewing   30

Lesson 16 Writing an Oral History: Writing the Report   32

Lesson 17 An Informative Speech: Research and Writing   34

UNDERSTANDING MAPS, CHARTS, AND GRAPHS

LESSON 18   Understanding Maps: How to Find Your Way   36

LESSON 19   Understanding Maps: A Population Map   38

LESSON 20   Understanding Maps: Political Maps   40

LESSON 21   Analyzing a Chart: Reporting on an Attitude Survey   42

LESSON 22   Analyzing a Graph: Explaining Facts and Trends   44

LESSON 23   Reading a Diagram: Explaining a Process   46

LESSON 24   Reading a Time Line: Explaining the Sequence of Events   48

SEPARATING BIAS, OPINION, AND FACT IN THE MEDIA

LESSON 25   Persuasive Writing: An Opinion Piece   50

LESSON 26   Detecting Bias: Careful Newspaper Reading   52

LESSON 27   Comparing Opinions: Newspaper Columnists   54

LESSON 28   Responding Critically: Mass Media   56

LESSON 29   Broadcast Journalism: Writing a Newscast   58

LESSON 30   Understanding Political Cartoons: Persuasive Techniques   60

LESSON 31   Understanding Current Events: Writing a Journal   62

APPLYING SOCIAL STUDIES SKILLS

LESSON 32   Writing Persuasively: Letter to the Editor   64

LESSON 33   Observing: What You Can Learn from a Photograph   66

LESSON 34   Observing: Propaganda and Fact   68

LESSON 35   Explaining History: Writing for Children   70

LESSON 36   Writing a Strategy: A Plan to Resolve a Conflict   72

LESSON 37   Writing to Inform: A Biography   74

WRITING CHECKLIST   75

To the Student

The writing skills that you learn in your social studies class will be useful throughout your life. When you analyze a chapter in a social studies book, you gain experience that you'll use when you think about a newspaper story or a television show or movie. In addition, learning how to write a speech will help you write and deliver an oral report at work.

The lessons in this book will give you a chance to practice a wide variety of writing styles and types. (See the Writing Checklist on page 75 for general help with writing.) You'll learn skills that will come in handy while you're in school, such as how to take notes and how to answer essay questions.

Writing in Social Studies is divided into six units that cover writing and social studies skills. There are also lessons that will help you improve your everyday writing.

Developing Social Studies Skills. In this unit, you'll practice taking notes so that you'll be able to remember the important information that you learn from books. This unit also shows you how to write your observations, analyze cause and effect, and answer essay questions.

Writing a Report. Writing a report is a great way to think about and understand a social studies topic. The lessons in this unit break down the steps a writer goes through to create a report. By the time you finish, you will know how to choose a topic, research it, write it, and revise it to create a polished paper.

Developing Listening and Speaking Skills. This unit will help you improve your listening and speaking skills through writing an oral history and an informative speech. You'll also practice taking notes when you listen to a speaker.

Understanding Maps, Charts, and Graphs. Maps, charts, and graphs help you see trends and percentages easily. Turning your understanding into words will allow you to communicate this information to others. In this unit, you'll write about population and political maps. You'll also analyze charts and graphs and explain diagrams and time lines.

Separating Bias, Opinion, and Fact in the Media. One of the most important skills you'll need in life is the ability to separate fact and opinion. In this unit, you'll analyze newscasts and newspapers to distinguish between bias and fact. You'll also write your own newscast and draw a political cartoon.

Applying Social Studies Skills. You use the writing skills you learn in social studies every day. In this unit, you'll write a letter to the editor, an observation of a photograph, a strategy for group cooperation, and a biography.

Writing about social studies can help you understand the world. The skills you gain will also be useful in your daily life. With practice, you can become a better writer. We hope that this book will help you learn this process.

LESSON 1
Taking Notes
Reading

What You'll LEARN

Taking notes from something you read isn't a skill you'll use only in school. Often, people take notes to help them in their jobs. For example, a worker in a fashion-design company might have to take notes from a magazine article to write a report about what's new in other designers' clothing lines.

What You'll DO

Use a chapter of a social studies book that you are using in your classroom to try this way of taking notes.

What You'll WRITE

Before you begin to take notes, skim what you're reading to find the general outline. To skim, look at the headings and subheadings. Then look at the pictures and graphs. Go back to the beginning and read the introduction. Then read the final paragraphs, which often summarize the chapter. Write your notes here.

1. What is the main topic of the chapter?

_____

_____

As you take notes, keep these tips in mind:

Write the name of the book and the number of the pages you are taking notes on at the top of the pages.

Don't write in sentences. Write important words or phrases.

Write the main points.

Write the supporting evidence for each point.

Be careful not to plagiarize, or copy exactly, a writer's ideas or words. Instead, write whose words or ideas they are. Writing generally known facts is not considered plagiarism.

2. What are the details or supporting evidence in the chapter?

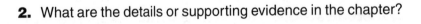

_____

_____

_____

_____

3. As you read, fill in these two pages. When you have finished, you should have a good idea of what is important in the reading you have just done. Select another chapter from the social studies book. Skim for main ideas and details.

Main point: _____

_____

_____

Supporting evidence: _____

_____

_____

_____

Main point: _____

_____

_____

Supporting evidence: _____

_____

_____

_____

Main point: _____

_____

_____

Supporting evidence: _____

_____

_____

_____

   If the chapter has more than three main points, use another piece of paper to complete your notes.

4. Go back over your notes. Underline the most important words. Use your notes to write a summary paragraph that explains what you learned in your reading.

_____

_____

_____

_____

LESSON 2 Using a Diagram Main Points and Supporting Details

What You'll LEARN Placing ideas into a diagram, or graphic organizer, can help you understand the key points and supporting information in a news article or a chapter of a social studies book.

What You'll DO Diagrams can show the connections among ideas. Here is one diagram that shows the main ideas and supporting details from an article about Florida history. Study the way this diagram is constructed.

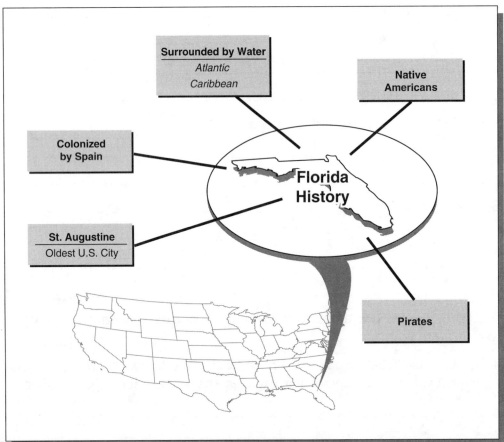

Notice that the main subject, Florida history, appears in the center circle. The article's main ideas are placed in circles attached to the center circle. Evidence and examples are listed below the main ideas.

What You'll WRITE Make a graphic organizer; then use it to write the main ideas and supporting details of an article or chapter you're reading.

1. Create a diagram that explains the main points of a chapter in a social studies textbook or an article. After you have finished, check your work against this list:

   ☐ Is the subject of the article or chapter in the center of the diagram?

   ☐ Are the main points in circles attached to the subject circle?

   ☐ Are supporting points or examples listed under each main point?

2. After you have finished your graphic organizer, use it to write a sentence or two that explains each main point in the chapter and the details that support it.

_____

_____

_____

_____

_____

_____

LESSON 3 Reading and Understanding Main Idea and Supporting Details

What You'll LEARN

You'll learn how to understand the main idea and supporting details when reading social studies texts.

What You'll DO

Read this article about resources in the Middle East. While you are reading, keep in mind that the main idea of a paragraph is often in the first sentence, which is called the *topic sentence*.

Also keep in mind that details often support the main idea. After you have answered the questions, write your own paragraph with a main idea and supporting details.

What You'll WRITE

Answer the questions that follow the reading.

> While the people of the Middle East know where national boundaries are, water resources do not. Middle Eastern peoples are forever joined through their need and use of water. Water for both Israel and Jordan comes from the same source. A dam built in one country may mean less water for another.
>
> It may be possible for the people of the Middle East to share their water. Some people from Turkey have recommended a "peace pipeline." This pipeline would bring precious water from northern Turkey to dry southern lands. Egypt might also share Nile River water with its neighbors.

1. What is the main idea of this passage? _____

_____

_____

2. What is the main idea of the first paragraph? _____

_____

_____

3. What details support this idea? _____

_____

_____

_____

4. What is the main idea of the second paragraph? _____

_____

_____

5. What details support this idea? _____

_____

_____

_____

_____

6. Look at the social studies book you have been studying. Choose a section that interests you. Plan a paragraph that summarizes this section. Include a topic sentence with a main idea and supporting details. Write your paragraph here.

_____

_____

_____

_____

_____

_____

_____

_____

_____

_____

_____

_____

_____

Reading and Understanding
LESSON **4** ## Analyzing
Cause and Effect

What You'll LEARN You'll learn how to recognize the causes and effects of events when you are reading social studies.

What You'll DO Read these passages. As you do, remember that the *cause* of something tells why it happens. The *effect* is the result of that cause.

What You'll WRITE Answer the questions that follow the reading.

> Finally, the East German government took action to prevent people from leaving that Communist country for freedom in West Berlin. At midnight on August 13, 1961, the East German government began to build the Berlin Wall. The concrete and barbed wire wall separated the two halves of the city for decades.
>
> The wall did its job. Only a handful of East Germans braved the guards on the towering structure to escape to the West. What the wall could not stop were the changes in the Soviet-backed East German government. The Soviets faced overwhelming trouble in their own country almost 30 years after the wall was built. As a result, their control over the Eastern European countries relaxed. By 1989, people in Eastern Europe had voted out Communist leaders. They opened trade and travel with the West. The wall, and all it stood for, collapsed.

1. What was a cause of the building of the Berlin Wall? _____

_____

_____

2. What was one effect of the building of the Wall? _____

_____

_____

3. What was a cause of the Soviet Union's loss of control over East Germany?

_____

_____

4. What were two effects of that loss of control? _____

_____

_____

Now read this passage from a social studies text and answer the questions that follow it.

> As many small farmers can tell you, it is difficult to compete with large corporate-owned farms. Some small farmers left the business. Others found ways around the power of the corporate farms. One way was to sign contracts with food processors so that all the farmers could produce. That meant the small farmers had a ready market. It also meant they knew how much money to expect for a harvest. Still other farmers found they could make ends meet by growing special crops on order.
>
> Another way small farmers managed to stay on their farms was to band together. They formed cooperatives— groups of farmers who became a unit. As a unit, they had power similar to that of the corporate farms. They could ensure the quality of their crops. They could bargain as a large group and get better prices for what they grew. Cooperatives sprang up around the country. California orange, grapefruit, and raisin farmers formed cooperatives. Florida citrus growers did too.

5. What is one cause of some farmers leaving farming? _____

_____

_____

6. What are three effects of small farmers being forced to compete with large, corporate-owned farms? _____

_____

_____

7. What is one effect of small farmers joining cooperatives? _____

_____

_____

_____

LESSON 5 Observing
Making Inferences

What You'll LEARN

By observing closely, you can learn to make inferences. Making an *inference* is sometimes called "reading between the lines." When you make an inference, you use what you already know to understand an idea that is not actually stated.

What You'll Do

Look at these two photographs of the Brooklyn Bridge in New York City. The photographs were taken about one hundred years apart. By looking closely at the differences between the two photographs, you can make inferences about what has happened in the city.

What You'll WRITE

After you have looked at the photos, answer the questions below.

1. What do you think has happened to New York City? _____

_____

_____

_____

_____

2. What inference can you make about what happened to the buildings in the time between the taking of each of the photographs? _____

_____

_____

_____

_____

_____

3. How do you think life might be different for the people who lived there during the changes?

_____

_____

_____

_____

_____

_____

4. Make an inference about the problems that might come with these changes.

_____

_____

_____

_____

_____

5. What benefits do you think might come from these changes? _____

_____

_____

_____

_____

_____

LESSON 6

Observing
Comparing and Contrasting

What You'll LEARN
In this lesson, you will learn how to compare and contrast what you see in a photograph. *Comparisons* show how things, events, or people are alike. *Contrasts* show how things, people, and events are different.

What You'll Do
Look at these photographs of villages in two different parts of the world. Then answer the questions to help you compare and contrast them.

What You'll WRITE After you have looked at the photos, answer the questions below. Think about how the two villages are similar and how they are different.

1. Compare the two villages. _____

_____

_____

_____

_____

2. Contrast the two villages. _____

_____

_____

_____

_____

3. Compare and contrast the villagers' homes in the two pictures. _____

_____

_____

_____

_____

4. Compare and contrast the land and the weather of the villages. _____

_____

_____

_____

_____

5. Compare and contrast the work the villagers do. _____

_____

_____

_____

_____

Answering Essay Questions
Strategies

LESSON 7

What You'll LEARN
Answering essay questions is a skill that you can learn. It is also a skill that you'll need in the future. You may be asked to write short essays on applications for college or for jobs. You will probably also have to write letters. When you write letters, you are writing essays.

What You'll DO
You are running for school board in your town or city. A local newspaper has sent out these questions to be answered by the candidates. As you look at the questions, keep in mind these tips for answering essay questions:

Read all of the question or questions before you begin to write your answers.

Plan your answer or answers to make sure that you include all of the information that is requested.

Be specific.

Unless the question asks for a list, write a topic sentence with the main idea. Back up the main idea with examples.

Know the code words in the following chart. When you see them in an essay test, they mean certain things.

Code Words	Meanings
describe means to	give details
explain means to	give the reasons
summarize means to	state the main points briefly
compare means to	mention similarities
contrast means to	mention differences
illustrate means to	give examples
discuss means to	think about all the angles of a topic
list means to	do exactly that—no details

What You'll WRITE Answer these questions as if you were running for the school board in your community.

1. What are some of the problems facing our schools?_____

_____

_____

_____

_____

2. What do you think the single biggest problem is? How would you solve it?

_____

_____

_____

3. Compare and contrast the quality of our schools with other schools in the area.

_____

_____

_____

_____

4. Summarize what you stand for. _____

_____

_____

_____

_____

5. Why do you think you would be a good school-board member? Explain your answer.

_____

_____

_____

_____

6. Are you a leader? Illustrate your answer with an example that shows your ability to lead.

_____

_____

_____

_____

8 Writing a Report
LESSON Choosing a Topic

What You'll LEARN   You will learn how to decide on a topic for a social studies report that is broad enough to be interesting, but narrow enough to be done.

What You'll DO   Read how one student decided on a report topic; then choose a topic for a report that you will write.

1. She knew she was interested in writing about the history of African Americans.

2. She researched the topic. She learned that whole books had been written about the history of African Americans, so the topic was too broad.

3. She thought about what interested her about the subject. She came up with these ideas: civil rights, civil rights in her town, and civil rights after World War II.

4. She went to the library. She found out that there was too much information about civil rights and too little about civil rights in her town. She chose the topic "Civil Rights After World War II" for her report.

What You'll WRITE   Answer these questions to help you decide on a topic.

1. What general topics am I interested in? _____

   a. _____

   b. _____

   c. _____

   d. _____

2. Which topic am I most interested in? Why? _____

_____

_____

_____

_____

3. How can I narrow this topic so that I will be able to write a research paper about it? (Go to the library to find out what information there is about your topic in books and magazines.)

a. _____

b. _____

c. _____

4. Choose the narrow topic that most interests you: _____

_____

5. Begin your research by listing books and magazine articles you will use as sources for your report. These sources are called the *bibliography*. If you will be using the *Readers' Guide to Periodical Literature*, follow these steps:

a. The *Guides* are listed by year. Check the years in which you think your subject may be mentioned.

b. Subjects are listed alphabetically. If there are no entries, try a related subject.

c. If the listing for your subject says *See* _____, look under the other term. If there are subheadings, look under the one closest to your topic.

d. Here is a typical entry with its parts explained:

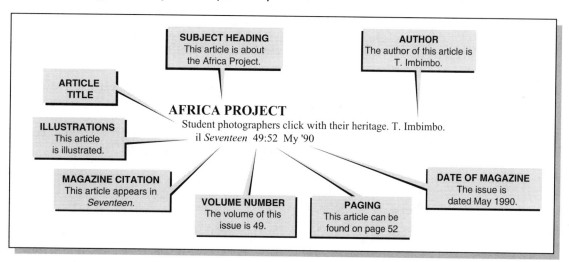

6. What are the three best sources for the information you want to include in your report? For a book, list name, author, publisher, city in which it was published, and year of publication. For a magazine, list the title, author, date it was published, and pages the information is on. This information will be important later when you write your bibliography.

_____

_____

_____

9 Writing a Report
LESSON
Taking Notes

What You'll LEARN
It's important to keep track of the information you're learning for your report. You'll also learn how to take notes that you can use to write your report.

What You'll DO
The easiest way to write a social studies report is to begin by organizing the information that you are learning. Taking good notes is important. If you don't, researching and writing a report can seem overwhelming.

What You'll WRITE
By answering the questions in this lesson, you will have outlined information from your first article or book. You can then use this information to help you write your report.

1. What questions do you want to answer in your report? _____

_____

_____

_____

You can use a notebook to write information for your report. Some writers find that taking notes on 3-inch by 5-inch cards is helpful. By doing this, they are able to put the cards in the order in which they want to use them when they write their report.

Writers who use this method often write a heading on the card to help them sort the cards. Here is one student's example:

cotton picker, mechanical   Jackson,
                                   "After the War" (p. 145)

When the mechanical cotton picker was invented, many African Americans left the South for the North because they lost their jobs. "Once again, African Americans found themselves without jobs and in desperation, headed North."

2. Skim the article or book. All of it may have to do with your topic, but you may only be interested in some of the information available. When you have found what you need, write the name of the book or article, the pages that were helpful, and a summary of what you have learned that will help you answer your question.

_____

_____

_____

_____

_____

_____

_____

3. What evidence or examples does the author give to back up what he or she is writing?

_____

_____

_____

_____

_____

_____

_____

_____

4. If an author writes an opinion that you want to include in your report, write it here exactly. Put quotation marks around the author's words. Also write the page on which the quotation appeared. If it was said by someone other than author, write that person's name also. _____

_____

_____

_____

_____

_____

_____

_____

10 Writing a Report
Creating an Outline

What You'll LEARN

Notes for a report need to be organized into an outline. This outline will help you write a first draft.

Looking at all the notes you've made for a report can be discouraging. How can you organize them so that they make sense?

What You'll DO

The first step is to read all of the information that you collected. After that, you'll sort the information into piles with similar ideas. That process will give you a rough organization for your report.

What You'll WRITE

Answer these questions to get your outline started.

1. Look at one of the piles. Write a sentence that describes its general topic.

_____

_____

2. Do the same thing for all the piles you made. On another piece of paper, write a topic sentence that describes each pile.

Now sort each pile into smaller groups by idea. For example, if the pile contains notes about the ways in which the invention of the cotton picker influenced the northward movement of African Americans, the smaller groups might be:

A. what African Americans did when they went North
B. how the North reacted to this population shift; and
C. what happened to the African Americans who stayed in the South

3. Write the ideas in one of your piles here. Then use another piece of paper to make a list for each pile. _____

_____

_____

_____

Now you can create an outline. At the top, write the statement that describes the topic of your report. Next, put your groups of information in order so that they support your topic. Write a main point for each of these groups. Under each of these, write phrases that support each main point.

Here is one student's outline:

Statement: After World War II, many African Americans moved to the cities. After that mass movement, the number of African Americans grew large enough to have a strong voice for civil rights and to begin to elect African American leaders.

I. Introduction
II. The move to the cities
    A. Mechanical cotton picker causes move
    B. What happened to African Americans in the cities

III. African Americans begin to gain civil rights in cities
    A. Treatment is bad in cities, causing African Americans to want change
    B. Enough people to work for civil rights in cities now
    C. African Americans begin to elect African American leaders to office

IV. Conclusion

Use this space to write your own outline, or use a separate piece of paper.

Statement:_____

_____

I. Introduction: _____

_____

II. _____
    A. _____
    B. _____

III. _____
    A. _____
    B. _____

IV. Conclusion: _____

_____

Writing a Report
The First Draft

What You'll LEARN You will learn to use your outline and notes to write a draft of your report.

What You'll DO Use the information you have gathered and organized to write your first draft.

What You'll WRITE Answer the questions on these pages to help you write your first draft.

The introduction. In a social studies report, this is the first paragraph. In the introduction, you include sentences that give a brief outline of what you will say in the report. The last sentence in the introduction should state the main idea of the paper, or what you are trying to prove.

Here is one student's introduction:

> When the mechanical cotton picker was invented in the 1940s, life changed for African Americans in the South. Suddenly, there were few jobs. As a result, large numbers of African Americans began to move North. Often, they were not treated well. They found they needed to organize to gain their civil rights. For the first time, African Americans began to elect other African Americans to office. This move of African Americans to the North helped make some major changes in United States society.

1. Use this space to write an introduction to your report.

_____

_____

_____

_____

_____

The body. For the main part of your report, or the body, it is useful to have your outline and notecards at hand. As you begin to write, follow your outline. Use the notes you made to help you write.

One important point to remember is not to plagiarize, or to copy exactly, someone's words or ideas without giving that person credit. It is fine to use facts that are generally known without saying where they came from, but if you use someone's exact words or ideas, quote the person.

As you make each point on your outline, make sure to include a topic sentence that explains your point. For example, in the body of her report about African Americans and civil rights after World War II, the student wrote this topic sentence:

> The prejudice and treatment that they found in the cities of the North caused many African Americans to want change.

2. Write the topic sentence for the first point you will make.

_____

_____

_____

Follow your topic sentence with evidence from your notes to back up your statement. For example, the sentence above might be followed with information or examples about the prejudice African Americans faced. You might include statements from people of the time about how they wanted things to change.

Conclusion. When you have made all the points you want to make in the body of your report, write the concluding paragraph. In this paragraph, you will summarize what you have shown in your report. Here is the student's conclusion to the report about civil rights and African Americans after World War II:

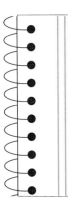

> African Americans moved to the cities after the mechanical cotton picker was invented because they needed work. Only when enough African Americans moved North and experienced prejudice did they begin to change things. For the first time, there were enough African Americans to elect other African Americans. Although these steps did not mean they had achieved equality, the people had begun the struggle that continues today.

3. Write your conclusion on another piece of paper.

12 Writing a Report
LESSON
Revising and Footnotes

What You'll LEARN Revising your work and writing the footnotes and bibliography are the final steps in creating a report.

What You'll Do By revising the draft, you have the chance to polish your work. Use this checklist to make your report stronger.

- ☐ Does your draft match your outline?
- ☐ Is your writing organized? Does one point lead to the next?
- ☐ Have you chosen the right words to say exactly what you mean?
- ☐ Have you checked your grammar?
- ☐ Have you proofread the report for spelling, capitalization, and punctuation?

Footnotes give credit to the writers whose ideas you are using in your report. They also give readers the ability to find out more or to check your sources. You use footnotes when you:

quote an author exactly;
use a writer's ideas;
use numbers or statistics.

You do not need to use footnotes when you write something that is common knowledge.

Footnotes are listed at the bottom of the page on which the information appears. If they are listed at the end of your report, they are called *endnotes*. They are numbered in order throughout the report. Here are the forms for different kinds of footnote sources:

A book:
[1] Jane Jackson, <u>After the War</u> (New York; Shanan Press, 1996), p. 39

A magazine article:
[2] Peter B. Neir, "The African American Vote," <u>Historical News</u>, March 1995, p. 22

A newspaper article:
[3] "The First Black Mayor," by Kelcy Argo, <u>Bedford Chronicle</u>, July 17, 1993

An article from an encyclopedia:
[4] "Cotton," <u>The Concise Columbia Encyclopedia</u>, 1983 ed., p. 202

If you use the same source more than once, you don't have to write all the information again. Instead, you write:

[5] Neir, p. 25

The *bibliography* belongs at the end of your report. In the bibliography, you list the sources you used for your report in alphabetical order. Here is a sample bibliography entry.

Argo, Kelcy. "The First Black Mayor," <u>Bedford Chronicle</u>, July 17, 1993

What You'll WRITE

Revise the draft, and prepare the footnote and bibliography.

1. Reread the draft of your report and revise it. Use the checklist on page 24 as a guide.

2. Write the first footnote for your report. _____

_____

3. Write your bibliography here. _____

_____

_____

_____

_____

_____

_____

4. Make a final copy of your report on a separate sheet of paper.

13 Writing a Report
LESSON
Creating an Essay Test

What You'll LEARN

Essay tests are a part of life. You can learn how to do them from the inside out—by writing your own.

What You'll DO

You'll be creating an essay test based on the report you just wrote. Here are some things to think about as you write your essay test. Remember that you're not thinking like a student now—you're thinking like a teacher. Here are some of the steps that teachers take when they create essay tests.

1. Teachers find out if a student understands the general sense of what the writer is saying by asking for a summary. This tells the teacher if the student understands the writer's main points.

2. An essay question may ask for examples that support a main point. This shows the teacher if the student is understanding the details.

3. Essay questions may also ask the student to go beyond the information in the report. The student may have to draw conclusions, make inferences, or predict outcomes. By doing this, students prove they can use the information they have read.

4. You have probably noticed that essay tests tend to proceed from the easiest to the most difficult questions. This can help focus students' thinking and lead them to handle harder questions.

5. Teachers use code words that mean specific things in an essay test. To understand some of the code words, see Essay Questions, in Lesson 7, Answering Essay Questions, on pages 14–15.

Code Words	Meanings
describe means to	give details
explain means to	give the reasons
summarize means to	state the main points briefly
compare means to	mention similarities
contrast means to	mention differences
illustrate means to	give examples
discuss means to	think about all the angles of a topic
list means to	do exactly that—no details

What You'll WRITE Write three essay questions on the lines below that will show whether students understand the main points and the details of your report. Write a question that will show whether students understand the importance of the information in your report. Also include a question that shows that students can use the information you have included to draw conclusions or make inferences about your topic. (See Lesson 5 to review making inferences.) Don't forget to include the answers to your questions.

1. _____

_____

_____

_____

Answer: _____

_____

_____

_____

2. _____

_____

_____

_____

Answer: _____

_____

_____

3. _____

_____

_____

_____

Answer: _____

_____

_____

_____

LESSON 14 Taking Notes
Listening

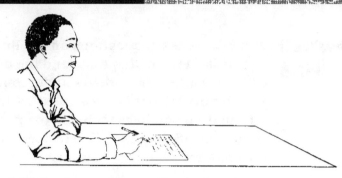

What You'll LEARN Taking notes while you listen is a skill that you will use throughout your life. At some point, for example, you may have to listen and then write directions to a place you've never visited. This activity will show you how to take good notes while you're listening to someone.

What You'll DO You might choose to fill in this outline while you are listening to a history or social studies lecture. You could also fill in these pages while you are listening to a television show about historical or current events.

What You'll WRITE Before the speaker begins, review this list of questions. Then fill in the blanks.

1. What is the topic? _____

_____

2. What do I already know about the topic? _____

_____

_____

_____

3. What is the speaker's purpose or the purpose of the presentation? _____

_____

_____

_____

4. What audience does the speaker intend to reach? _____

_____

_____

5. What information do I hope to learn? _____

_____

_____

_____

As you listen to the speaker or the presentation, keep the following questions in mind. Fill in the answers as you hear them.

6. What's the point of the presentation?
(Speakers often announce their purpose by saying things like "I want to tell you about …") _____

_____

_____

_____

_____

_____

7. What are the key points that the speaker is making?
(You can tell when a speaker is making an important point when he or she uses phrases like "There are three reasons …") _____

_____

_____

_____

_____

_____

8. What supporting evidence does the speaker give for each key point?
Write the evidence for each point the speaker makes. _____

_____

_____

_____

_____

_____

9. At the end of a presentation, a speaker usually restates the important information. How does the speaker summarize his or her speech? _____

_____

_____

_____

_____

_____

15 Writing an Oral History
LESSON
Interviewing

What You'll LEARN
In an oral history, people tell what happened to them during their lives. An oral history can often tell us a great deal about what life was like at different times. You'll learn how to interview a person for an oral history in this activity.

What You'll DO
Choose a person whom you think has had an interesting life. Then write a series of questions that will help you find out more about his or her life. If you want some additional ideas about the questions to ask, see the next activity, Writing an Oral History.

Here are some tips about writing interview questions for an oral history:

Ask the basic questions first.

Ask your questions so that they lead from one to the next. That will help the interview go more smoothly.

Ask questions that cover the important things that happened in the person's life or that cover the important events the person lived through.

Ask the person if there is anything you didn't ask that he or she would like to talk about.

If you are unsure about an answer that was given, repeat what you have in your notes and ask if that is correct.

Here are one student's interview questions:

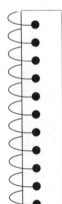

1. Please spell your name.
2. What is your age?
3. When were you born?
4. Where were you born?
5. Where have you lived?
6. Tell me about your hometown.
7. What do you remember most happily about your childhood?

What You'll WRITE Use the following spaces to write the questions you will ask. When you go on the interview, you can write the answers in the space. You might also want to write the questions on the first page of a small notepad and the answers in the rest of the notebook. Be sure to write exactly what the person says, using his or her own words. You can also record the answers on videotape or audiotape, if you get permission from the person first. After the interview, listen to the tape and write exactly what the person said.

Question 1: _____

_____

_____

Answer: _____

_____

_____

_____

_____

Question 2: _____

_____

_____

Answer: _____

_____

_____

_____

_____

Question 3: _____

_____

_____

Answer: _____

_____

_____

_____

_____

16 Writing an Oral History
LESSON Writing the Report

What You'll LEARN
You'll learn how to take the notes from your interview and turn them into a written report.

What You'll DO
An oral history is usually written in the words of the person you interview. However, most interviews are too long to write every word. Also, many times people say things more than once. They may also say things that are not about the subject. Sometimes, people don't remember things in order. Your job is to take the notes and turn them into an interesting story. You will also need to write what the person said so that it follows the events of his or her life. If you find that you don't have answers to many of the questions, ask the person if you can interview him or her again.

What You'll WRITE
First, review your notes. Underline or highlight the most interesting things that the person has said. To help you write your report, answer these questions. Then write your final report on another piece of paper. Try to think of an unusual or creative beginning for your story, such as: What would life be like without television?

1. What is the person's name? _____

2. When and where was the person born? _____
_____

3. Describe the person's early life. How was it different from the way we live now?
_____
_____
_____
_____

4. What does the person remember about going to school? How much education did the person have? _____
_____
_____
_____

5. What did the person do after he or she finished school? _____

_____

_____

6. What jobs has the person had? _____

_____

_____

7. What important events in history does the person remember? What was the person doing at those times? _____

_____

_____

_____

8. What does the person think are the most important things that happened in his or her life?

_____

_____

_____

_____

9. Why are those things important? _____

_____

_____

_____

_____

10. What are the biggest changes the person has seen in his or her life? _____

_____

_____

_____

11. Would the person change any of the choices he or she made in life? Why?

_____

_____

_____

_____

17 An Informative Speech
Research and Writing

LESSON

What You'll LEARN
Writing a speech, or an oral report, has some things in common with writing a report. There are some things that are different about giving a speech, though. In this activity, you'll learn what those differences are.

What You'll DO
Reread the unit about writing a social studies report, on pages 16–25. Like a written report, a speech has to have a narrow topic. A speech also must have details that support the main point.

What You'll WRITE
Before you work on your speech, answer these questions:

1. How long do I want my speech to be? _____

2. Who are my listeners? What are their interests and experiences?

_____

_____

Answer these questions to help put your speech together:

3. How could I relate my topic to their interests? _____

_____

_____

_____

_____

4. What is the main point (or points) I want to make? _____

_____

_____

5. What facts support my main point (or points)? _____

_____

_____

_____

_____

_____

6. When you write a speech, illustrate your main points with true stories that will keep your audience interested. For example, if you are making the point that life was difficult for Japanese Americans during World War II, you might make your point by using a story about a Japanese-American girl's experience in an internment camp. Write a story you will use here. _____

_____

_____

_____

_____

_____

_____

_____

_____

_____

_____

7. Write an outline for your speech. Use the information in Lesson 10, Writing a Report: Creating an Outline, to help you.

Many people who give speeches use index cards. After they write their speech, they write words that remind them of their points and supporting evidence on separate index cards. That way, they can find their place in their speech.

After you write your speech, practice it. As funny as it sounds, a good place to practice your speech is in front of the bathroom mirror. As you practice it, use this checklist:

- ❏ Does my speech flow from point to point?
- ❏ Are my sentences fairly short and easy to understand?
- ❏ Do I look directly at people in the audience as I speak?
- ❏ Do I speak loudly, slowly, and clearly enough to be heard?
- ❏ Do I use gestures to help make my points?
- ❏ If I am using pictures or other visual aids, are they ready and in order. Are they big enough for the audience to see? (Don't pass out visual aids while you are talking.)
- ❏ Have I practiced my speech enough to be comfortable giving it?

LESSON 10

Understanding Maps
How to Find Your Way

What You'll LEARN

Often, people use maps to explain how to travel somewhere. After this exercise, you will be able to use a map to describe a route to someone.

What You'll Do

Look at these maps of Harrisburg, Pennsylvania. The *legend*, which explains the maps' symbols, is underneath.

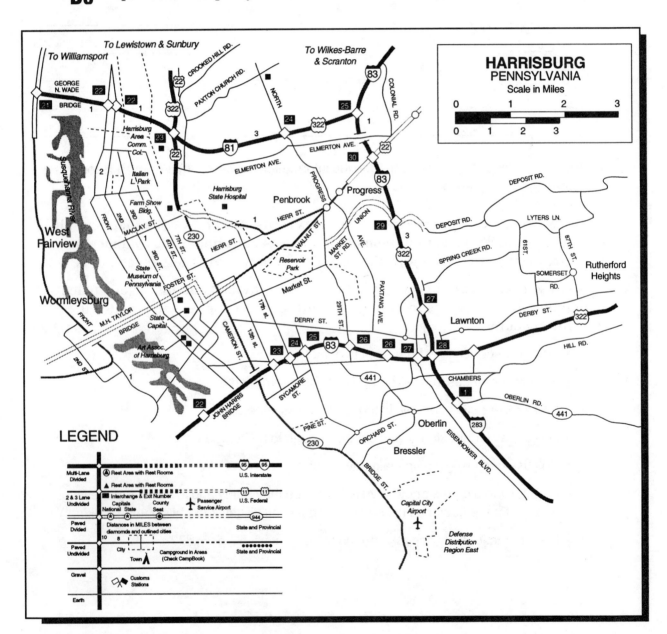

What You'll Write directions for two visitors based on the maps you've just studied.

WRITE **1.** Your friend is visiting from New York City. He's calling from a phone booth at exit 23 on U.S. Interstate 81. Write how he can get to your house, which is in Rutherford Heights, at the intersection of Lyters Lane and 87th. First, trace the route on the map. Then, after you are sure of the route, write the directions. Tell your friend whether he is to turn left or right and in what direction he will be traveling. _____

_____

_____

_____

_____

_____

_____

_____

2. Another friend is coming in from the airport and wants to rent a car and see the Susquehanna River from the north side. She's asked you to map a route that keeps her on the streets closest to the river, all the way until she crosses over the George N. Wade Bridge and heads to Williamsport. Write the directions that she will use to reach her destination.

_____

_____

_____

_____

_____

_____

_____

3. How did the legend help you give accurate directions?_____

_____

_____

_____

19 Understanding Maps
LESSON A Population Map

What You'll LEARN You'll learn to describe what a map shows about the population density of the world.

What You'll Do Analyze the map below. Look at the legend to understand what the different shadings mean.

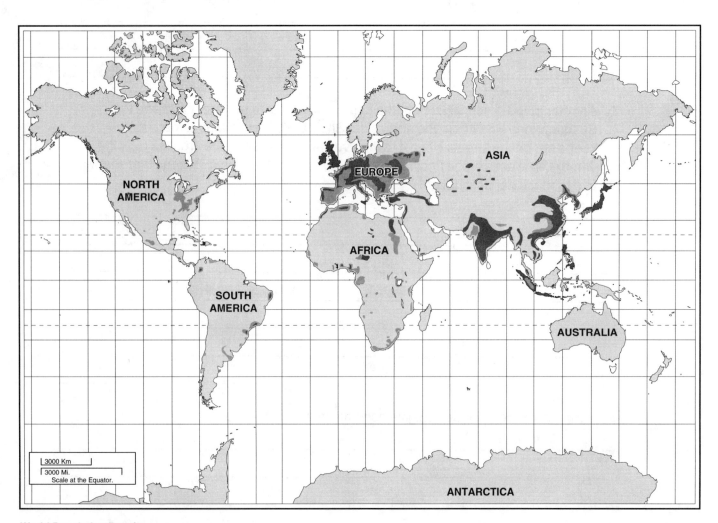

World Population Density

 0-60 people per square mile

61-125 people per square mile

Over 125 people per square mile

What You'll WRITE Answer these questions based on what you read on the map. Use complete sentences.

1. Write a paragraph comparing and contrasting the population density of North and South America. Include which country is more densely settled and where population tends to cluster in each continent. _____

_____

_____

_____

_____

_____

2. Compare this population map with a political map of the world. If you were planning a 12-stop international tour and wanted to see the largest number of people possible, where would you go? _____

_____

_____

_____

3. Compare this map with a world political map. Which countries in Europe have the least dense populations? Infer, or make a good guess about, why this might be the case.

_____

_____

_____

_____

4. Describe which areas on the map tend to have the smallest population density. Make an inference, or a logical guess, about why this is so. _____

_____

_____

_____

_____

LESSON 20 Understanding Maps
Political Maps

What You'll LEARN

You'll learn to analyze political maps and answer questions about them.

What You'll DO

Look at these two maps of the Middle East in the 1910s and in the 1980s. Notice the legend for the Middle East of the 1910s.

**Middle East
1910s**

**Middle East
1980s**

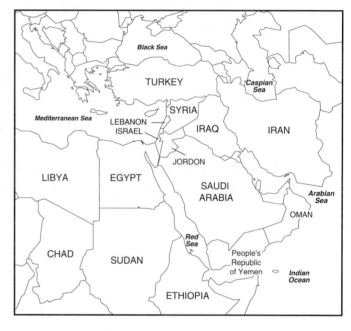

■	British
▥	Italian
▤	Ottoman
▨	Russian
▦	Independent

What You'll WRITE

Compare and contrast the two maps from the previous page. Answer in complete sentences the questions that follow.

1. What countries were formed from the lands that were independent in the 1910s?

_____

_____

_____

_____

_____

2. What second language are the citizens of Egypt likely to speak? Why did you make this inference, or logical guess? _____

_____

_____

_____

_____

3. Make an inference about why the Ottomans might have wanted the area of the Middle East that has a coastline on the Red Sea, rather than in the center of what is now Saudi Arabia. _____

_____

_____

_____

4. What countries of the 1980s might have an interest in making sure the Mediterranean Sea does not become polluted? Explain your answer. _____

_____

_____

_____

5. Which Middle Eastern countries have the largest number of borders to protect? Infer how this might affect these countries. _____

_____

_____

_____

_____

LESSON 21
Analyzing a Chart
Reporting on an Attitude Survey

What You'll LEARN You can look at the numbers on a chart and use them to understand a subject.

What You'll Do Study this chart. It shows the results of a survey of attitudes about a community. Of the town's 1,000 residents, 678 responded to the survey. The chart shows the percentage of people who answered each question. Your job is to report on the survey results to the city council.

Question	yes (%)	no (%)	don't know (%)
Do you think the city is going in the right direction?	34	54	12
Would you re-elect the members of the city council?	45	45	10
What is the biggest threat facing the city?			
Crime?	47		
Drug use?	15		
School system?	23		
Pollution?	15		
What is the best thing about the city?			
Location	23		
Good schools	18		
Friendly people	34		
Good city facilities	14		
Safe city	12		
Do you feel the city is well run?	34	54	12
Does the city respond to your needs?	24	66	10
Would you recommend that a friend move here?	32	40	28

What You'll WRITE

Remember that you are explaining the results to the city council. Write a memo to the members of the council. Explain the results of the survey and what you think the council should know. (What do people in your city seem most concerned about? What are they happy with?) Then suggest how the council should respond to the survey, including what action it might take.

MEMO

TO: Members of City Council

FROM: _____

RE: Survey Results

_____
_____
_____
_____
_____
_____
_____
_____
_____
_____
_____
_____
_____
_____
_____
_____
_____
_____
_____
_____
_____
_____
_____
_____

Analyzing a Graph
Explaining Facts and Trends

LESSON 22

What You'll LEARN You'll use the information in graphs to explain the information that is shown in picture form.

What You'll DO Below are two graphs that explain some facts about immigration to the United States. Look at the information and answer the questions on the next page.

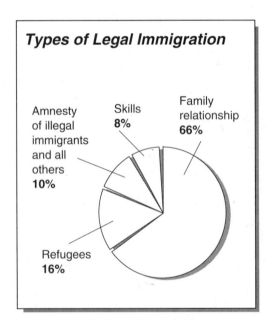

Types of Legal Immigration

Amnesty of illegal immigrants and all others **10%**

Skills **8%**

Family relationship **66%**

Refugees **16%**

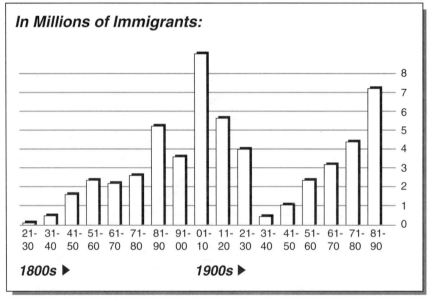

In Millions of Immigrants:

21-30 31-40 41-50 51-60 61-70 71-80 81-90 91-00 01-10 11-20 21-30 31-40 41-50 51-60 61-70 71-80 81-90

8
7
6
5
4
3
2
1
0

1800s ▶   *1900s* ▶

What You'll WRITE Use the graphs above to answer these questions. Use complete sentences in your answers.

1. How does legal immigration in the 1800s compare with legal immigration in the 1900s?

_____

_____

_____

2. Contrast the reasons that legal immigrants are allowed into the United States.

_____

_____

_____

_____

_____

3. Draw a conclusion about future immigration if the current trend continues.

_____

_____

_____

_____

_____

4. Use the circle graph to argue the point that the United States has little control over the people who immigrate to the country.

_____

_____

_____

_____

_____

5. Use the circle graph to argue the point that the United States's immigration policy is designed to reunite families.

_____

_____

_____

_____

6. Look at the bar graph and write whether you think the current upward trend of immigration to the United States will continue. Explain your answer.

_____

_____

_____

_____

_____

23 Reading a Diagram
LESSON
Explaining a Process

What You'll LEARN A *diagram* shows steps in a process or how something (a company, for example) is organized. Often, people have to read diagrams to find out how to get something done.

What You'll DO Look at this diagram. It explains how cases reach the U.S. Supreme Court. At each level of the process, the side that disagrees with the decision of the court may appeal the court's decision to the next court level.

How Cases Reach the Supreme Court

U.S. SUPREME COURT

Highest State Court
(Last court that can be appealed to in a state.)

U.S. Courts of Appeals
(12 courts that review cases from their U.S. district.)

U.S. Courts of Appeals for the Federal Circuit
(Court that handles appeals in patent cases and cases involving international trade. Reviews civil cases against the U.S. government.)

State Appellate Courts
(Courts that review cases from state trial courts)

4 U.S. District Courts
(Courts that handle federal criminal and civil cases.)

U.S. District Court of International Trade
(Court that handles cases that involve imports.)

U.S. Claims Court
(Court that handles federal cases involving over $10,000, and cases concerning agreements with Native Americans.)

State Trial Courts
(Courts that try civil and criminal cases. Some cases may begin in city or county courts.)

What You'll WRITE

Answer these questions, explaining each step in the process. Use complete sentences.

1. You are advising the members of a Native American nation on their land-rights case. They have asked you to describe the process through which their case will go if they lose at every level and continue to file appeals. _____

_____

_____

_____

_____

_____

_____

2. A convicted bank robber thinks that he was convicted under an unjust law. You are his lawyer. He wants to know, in writing, what course his case could take if he continues to appeal it. _____

_____

_____

_____

_____

_____

_____

_____

3. An importer was convicted of unfair trade practices. He wants to know what will happen if his company keeps fighting the conviction. Remember to compose your answer so that someone from another country, who does not know U.S. law, can understand the process. _____

_____

_____

_____

_____

_____

_____

_____

24 Reading a Time Line
LESSON
Explaining the Sequence of Events

What You'll LEARN From looking at a time line, you can see when events happened during the course of history. You can reconstruct the sequence in which the events happened.

What You'll Do Look at this time line about the Korean War.

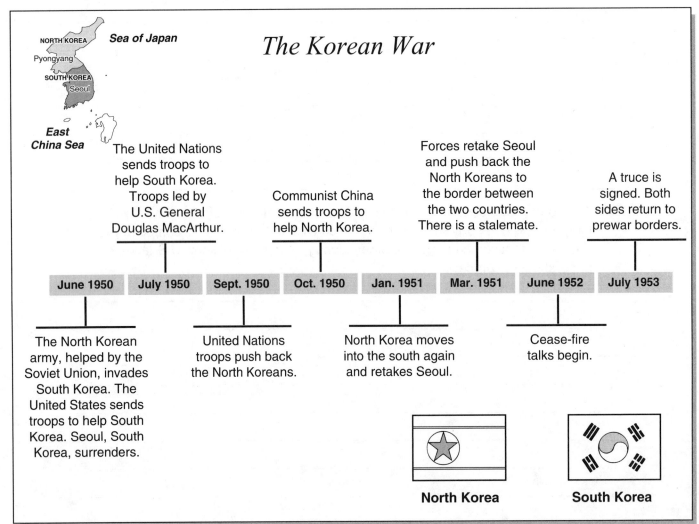

The Korean War

NORTH KOREA — Sea of Japan
Pyongyang
SOUTH KOREA
Seoul

East China Sea

The United Nations sends troops to help South Korea. Troops led by U.S. General Douglas MacArthur.

Communist China sends troops to help North Korea.

Forces retake Seoul and push back the North Koreans to the border between the two countries. There is a stalemate.

A truce is signed. Both sides return to prewar borders.

| June 1950 | July 1950 | Sept. 1950 | Oct. 1950 | Jan. 1951 | Mar. 1951 | June 1952 | July 1953 |

The North Korean army, helped by the Soviet Union, invades South Korea. The United States sends troops to help South Korea. Seoul, South Korea, surrenders.

United Nations troops push back the North Koreans.

North Korea moves into the south again and retakes Seoul.

Cease-fire talks begin.

North Korea

South Korea

What You'll Answer these questions. Use complete sentences.
WRITE

1. Describe the movement of North Korean troops during the war. _____

_____

_____

_____

_____

2. Describe how United Nations forces responded to the North Korean invasion
of South Korea. _____

_____

_____

_____

_____

3. When did China enter the war? Why do you think China chose that time to
enter the war? _____

_____

_____

_____

_____

4. Which year do you think was the most important in the war? Explain your answer.

_____

_____

_____

_____

5. Infer what happened between March 1951 and June 1952. Explain your answer.

_____

_____

_____

_____

_____

_____

25 Persuasive Writing
An Opinion Piece

What You'll LEARN

Writing can be used to persuade people of your point of view. Writers do this every day in the opinion pages of the newspaper. You'll have a chance to write your own opinion piece in this exercise.

What You'll Do

Read these statements about irradiated food. Then decide what position you want to take on the issue. Write an opinion piece designed to persuade people that your point of view is the most reasonable one.

Irradiated food is food exposed to radiation to kill harmful bacteria.

Many scientists believe that irradiation is a safe way to keep food from spoiling quickly. It also kills organisms that cause diseases.

Other scientists believe that irradiation robs food of some of its nutrition. They also believe that it may cause cancer and birth defects.

Maine has banned irradiated food. New York and New Jersey have delayed its use.

Growers say that irradiation allows them to ship their food to more markets that are farther away. They also say that irradiation means less spoilage.

Environmental groups have threatened to boycott stores that sell irradiated produce.

Professor of Environmental Medicine, Dr. Samuel Epstein, says that not enough studies have been done to make sure that irradiated food is safe.

Dr. Frank Lu of the World Health Organization believes that these fears are groundless. He says that irradiation reduces the number of harmful organisms in food and makes it healthier.

Protesters say that there is no way to know if irradiated food, such as strawberries, will be used for purposes such as jelly. Fresh irradiated strawberries must be labeled. Those used in processed foods might not be labeled.

The Food and Drug Administration approved irradiated food after looking at 441 studies and deciding that the procedure was safe.

What You'll WRITE Write an opinion piece about irradiated foods. Remember to start with an introduction that tells your opinion. Then write your reasons, backed up with supporting evidence. Finish with a conclusion that will persuade people that your view is correct.

_____

_____

_____

_____

_____

_____

_____

_____

_____

_____

_____

_____

_____

_____

_____

_____

_____

_____

_____

_____

_____

_____

_____

_____

_____

_____

LESSON 26 Detecting Bias
Careful Newspaper Reading

What You'll LEARN
Good readers read everything with a critical eye. Newspaper readers are no exception. In this exercise, you will read a newspaper story for bias.

What You'll DO
Read this newspaper article. While you are reading, be alert for bias. Think about how to tell a fact from an opinion. Remember that:

A *fact* is a statement that can be proven to be true.

An *opinion* is what someone believes.

Bias is an attempt to present opinions as facts.

Former Criminal to Run Company

NEW TOWN—Frank Stewart reached a longtime goal yesterday when he was named president of Argon Enterprises.

"It's a great day for me, and a great day for the company," Stewart, Argon's vice president, said yesterday.

Stewart's foes, who insist that he is a criminal, say that he has no place running a business, and they might be right. "The guy's a crook. He bought his way out of jail, and now he's trying to buy respectability," said Andrew Johnson, who lost his battle to remain as president.

Johnson said that Stewart bribed company officers to vote him into the job. He added that Stewart will turn the company into a front for criminals. Stewart has spent time in federal prison for criminal activity.

"Mr. Johnson should be careful," Stewart threatened the company's former president.

What You'll
WRITE
Answer these questions based on the story you've just read. Use complete sentences.

1. What is an example of fact you learned from the article? _____
    _____
    _____

2. What is an example of opinion you learned from the article? _____
    _____
    _____
    _____
    _____

3. Find an example of bias in the article. Write the example here and explain why you think that it is biased. _____
    _____
    _____
    _____
    _____
    _____

4. Rewrite the article so that it is not biased. _____
    _____
    _____
    _____
    _____
    _____
    _____
    _____
    _____
    _____
    _____
    _____
    _____
    _____

27 Comparing Opinions
LESSON **Newspaper Columnists**

What You'll LEARN
The editorial pages of newspapers and news magazines often contain opinion pieces. By learning to compare these opinions, you can become better informed.

What You'll DO
Find two columns that have differing views on the same subject. Read both columns carefully. Remember that you will be comparing and contrasting their views. Read critically. Consider whether opinions are given as facts. Question whether something that is given as a fact really is a fact. Also look for these errors in reasoning:

Too-broad generalizations: "All teenagers are loud."

Incorrectly linking causes and effects: "Because you were sleeping, the dog ran away."

Attacking a person instead of dealing with the question: "He is a liar. His beliefs on schools are wrong."

What You'll WRITE
After you have read the newspaper columns, answer these questions. Use complete sentences.

1. What is columnist number 1's argument? _____

_____

_____

_____

_____

_____

2. What facts does columnist number 1 use to support his or her position?

_____

_____

_____

_____

_____

3. What is columnist number 2's argument? _____

_____

_____

_____

_____

4. What facts does columnist number 2 use to support his or her position? _____

_____

_____

_____

_____

_____

5. Compare the two columnists' styles. Which do you prefer? Why? _____

_____

_____

_____

_____

_____

6. Do you see errors in reasoning in either column? Explain. _____

_____

_____

_____

_____

_____

7. Explain which columnist you find more convincing, and why. _____

_____

_____

_____

_____

_____

_____

28 Responding Critically
Mass Media

LESSON 28

What You'll LEARN
You can learn to be more critical of the news you read and see. This activity will show you how.

What You'll DO
You'll take notes after reading the major stories in the newspaper and watching a TV newscast. Then you'll compare what you heard and read.

What You'll WRITE
Write the answers to these questions in your notebook. Then answer the questions on the next page.

1. What are the main stories in the newspaper?

   In a newspaper, the major stories are usually on the front page. The most important of these stories are usually at the top of the page with larger headlines.

2. What are the main stories in the TV newscast?

   Often, the most important stories are told first. Sometimes, though, the most important stories are told after stories that have exciting pictures. For example, a house fire might make a dramatic story but be much less important than a bill passed by Congress.

3. Analyze the major story of the day in the newspaper and on TV. List what you learned about the story from each source. Which gives you more information, the newscast or the newspaper?

4. What advantages does the newspaper have in covering this story? What advantages does the newscast have in covering this story?

5. To which parts of the story did the newspaper give more importance? To which parts of the story did the TV newscast give more importance?

6. Which coverage do you think is more believable? Explain your answer.

7. Did you find any bias in either the newspaper or the TV? Explain your answer.

8. What questions would you like to have answered that the newscast did not answer? What questions would you like to have answered that the newspaper story did not answer?

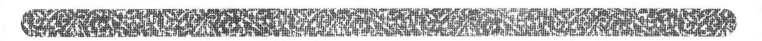

After you have taken notes about the newscast and the newspaper coverage, answer these questions:

9. Which of the media do you think provides better information? Explain your answer.

_____

_____

_____

_____

10. Which of the media do you trust more? Explain your answer. _____

_____

_____

_____

_____

11. What advantages do newspapers have over TV broadcasts? _____

_____

_____

_____

_____

12. What advantages does television coverage have over newspaper coverage?

_____

_____

_____

_____

13. Think of an event that has happened recently in your school or in your community. On the lines below, write briefly how you would report the story in a newspaper and on TV.

_____

_____

_____

_____

_____

_____

_____

_____

29 Broadcast Journalism
Writing a Newscast

LESSON

What You'll LEARN

There is an art to writing the news for broadcast. In this activity, you will try your hand at television news.

What You'll DO

First, choose a historical event that you have been studying on which you will report. Take notes on what you think is important about this event. Remember that a big part of TV news can be the picture that viewers are watching. Think about what pictures you want to include in your newscast.

Use the tips on this page as a guide to writing your newscast.

Keep in mind the most important information that you want people to know about this story. Stories on TV news are often no more than a minute long.

Use active words.

Use short, simple sentences that viewers can follow.

Capturing viewers' attention at the beginning of the story is important. You can do this by telling the most important facts first, if the news is important and new. You can also start with an interesting story or fact.

Describe the pictures or news footage that will appear behind the newscaster. Is your piece a voiceover (the viewer only hears the voice and sees photographs about the story)? Is your piece one in which the reporter is speaking with a still picture behind his or her head? Is the story one in which there are no pictures?

Do not include bias in your report. Opinions should be voiced by experts, not by you.

If there are two sides in your story, include both.

After you present both sides, let the viewer draw his or her own conclusion.

What You'll WRITE Write your newscast on this page. Tell what pictures or videos you will use. Make sure that your story is one minute long. You can read it to yourself to find out how long it is.

Newscast

_____

Pictures

_____

30 Understanding Political Cartoons
LESSON
Persuasive Techniques

What You'll LEARN
Political cartoons comment on the news. Cartoonists use exaggeration, satire, and humor to get their points across. Most try to influence the reader to think in a certain way. In this activity, you will analyze and respond to political cartoons.

What You'll DO
Analyze these cartoons to understand the cartoonists' views and the ways in which they communicate them.

What You'll WRITE
Answer the questions under the cartoon and on the next page. Use complete sentences in your answers.

1. What is the cartoonist trying to say in the cartoon above?_____

_____

_____

_____

2. How does the cartoonist use art to make a point? _____

_____

_____

_____

_____

3. What other techniques does the artist use to get a message across? _____

_____

_____

_____

_____

4. How does this cartoonist feel about the national debt? _____

_____

_____

_____

5. What techniques does the artist use to make a point? _____

_____

_____

_____

_____

Understanding Current Events
Writing a Journal

What You'll LEARN By tracking what happens with a controversial issue, you will understand how the issue develops. You will also understand how newspaper coverage influences what you think about an issue.

What You'll DO Choose an issue that interests you and is likely to be in the news every day. You'll keep a current-events journal of what happens about that issue. Then you'll write what you think might happen next.

What You'll WRITE Set aside part of a notebook in which to keep your journal. Here is a sample of the questions you should answer in your journal every day. Notice that the list includes the 5Ws.

Fill in these two pages on the first day. Then answer the questions in your notebook daily for as long as your teacher requests. Use complete sentences in your writing.

1. What happened today?

Who? _____

What? _____

When? _____

Where? _____

Why? _____

_____

2. Why is this event important? _____

_____

_____

_____

_____

_____

_____

_____

_____

3. One fact that I learned today: _____

_____

_____

_____

4. One opinion that I read today: _____

_____

_____

_____

5. What questions about this event do I still have? _____

_____

_____

_____

6. What do I think might be the next thing that happens regarding this issue?

_____

_____

_____

_____

_____

7. How might someone's actions affect what happens next?_____

_____

_____

_____

_____

_____

_____

_____

32 Writing Persuasively
LESSON
Letter to the Editor

What You'll LEARN

Writing a letter to the editor is one of the ways that citizens can voice their opinions. You'll practice this skill in the following activity.

What You'll DO

Choose a subject that is in the news and that you have strong feelings about. You might choose to comment on a bill that would cut funding for school sports. You might choose to voice your opinion about the way dogs are kept in the local pound. Whatever topic you choose, it should be of interest to people in your community. Remember: someone may read it and take action.

Here are some hints about organizing your letter.

Clearly state your opinion at the beginning of the letter.

Support your opinion with facts.

Make sure your points follow logically. You might want to make a brief outline first.

Conclude by restating your main point. You may also want to suggest a course of action.

Here are some strategies to make your letter more effective.

Write about something that is in the news right now. An editor is unlikely to publish a letter about something that no longer matters to people.

Keep your tone reasonable. That will help convince readers that your suggestions are workable.

Check your newspaper's editorial page for guidelines about the letters the paper accepts.

Read your newspaper's editorial page to see examples of letters that have been published from community members.

Use the opening "To the Editor:"

Make sure that you print your name, address, and phone number on the letter. Also sign the letter.

What You'll WRITE Use this page to write your letter. When you have finished, proofread and revise your letter; then copy it or type it on another page and send it to a newspaper.

To the Editor:

_____

_____

_____

_____

_____

_____

_____

_____

_____

_____

_____

_____

_____

_____

_____

_____

_____

_____

_____

_____

_____

_____

_____

_____

_____

_____

LESSON 33 Observing What You Can Learn from a Photograph

What You'll LEARN
By closely studying a photograph, you can learn important information. You can also use this information to write captions.

What You'll DO
Carefully observe this picture. It was taken by Lewis W. Hine in 1912 and shows children at work in a cannery.

What You'll WRITE

Captions can be written for several purposes.

1. Imagine that this picture is being used to inform people about child labor in 1912. Use the information you know about this picture and the inferences you can make about what is happening in the photograph to write a caption. _____

_____

_____

_____

_____

_____

2. Imagine that this photograph is being used to persuade people to make sure that child labor laws are kept in force. Write a caption that persuades people of the importance of child labor laws. _____

_____

_____

_____

_____

_____

3. Imagine that this photograph is part of a book about the artistry of the photographer, Lewis W. Hine. Write a caption that describes why the photograph is included in this book.

_____

_____

_____

_____

_____

4. Imagine that this photograph is one that you found in your family's belongings. There is a note that the girl in the center of the photograph is a relative. Write a caption in which you tell family members about this photograph. _____

_____

_____

_____

_____

_____

LESSON 34 Observing Propaganda and Fact

What You'll LEARN Are you aware of people who want to influence what you think? Creating your own propaganda (spreading ideas and rumors to help or hurt a cause) will help you understand how people try to influence you.

What You'll DO Look at this etching of African American slaves working at a cotton gin around the time of the Civil War in the United States.

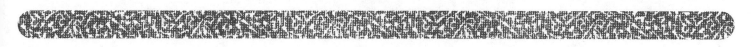

What You'll WRITE

Write three captions for the etching on the previous page.

1. Write this caption objectively. Describe who the people are and what they are doing.

_____

_____

_____

_____

_____

_____

_____

2. Imagine that you are writing a caption for a newspaper published in the South during the Civil War. Think about how to write this caption to make people as sympathetic to your side as possible. _____

_____

_____

_____

_____

_____

_____

_____

_____

3. Imagine that you are writing a caption for a newspaper published in the North during the Civil War. Think about how to write the caption to make people as sympathetic to your side as possible. _____

_____

_____

_____

_____

_____

_____

_____

35 Explaining History
Writing for Children

What You'll LEARN

One of the important skills in social studies is explaining what you know. On these pages, you'll explain an important historical event in a picture book so that a first-grader can understand it.

What You'll DO

First, choose a topic that interests you or that you are studying. Here are some possibilities:

the Boston Tea Party
a biography of an important person
the history of books
the story of an explorer and his or her discovery
the struggle for civil rights

Research your topic. Take notes about what you discover. Then organize what you have learned into a story that a first-grader can understand. Write possible ways to illustrate each page.

What You'll WRITE

1. On the rest of this page, use a graphic organizer to plan the flow of ideas in your book. (Graphic organizers are drawings that can help you organize your information. For examples of graphic organizers, refer to Lesson 2, Using a Diagram; Lesson 23, Reading a Diagram; and Lesson 24, Reading a Time Line.)

2. Make a thumbnail sketch (a small version of the pages in your book) on this page. Write the words as they would appear. Also write what illustrations or drawings you would use. If you need more pages, use another piece of paper.

After you've finished your thumbnail sketch, make a full-size book. Give it to a first-grader to see if he or she understands what you wrote.

36 Writing a Strategy
LESSON
A Plan to Resolve a Conflict

What You'll LEARN
You can use your skills to create a plan to resolve a conflict.

What You'll DO
Sometimes, people have to solve problems close to home. For example, conflicts sometimes develop between groups of people in a school. Imagine that you have been given the job of planning a strategy to help two groups of people to get along. Right now, the two groups of students refuse to talk to one another. Each accuses the other of starting the fight by making negative remarks. Both groups have been heard making negative remarks. Lately, members of the two groups have been in fights in the halls.

What You'll WRITE
Answer these questions to help you plan a strategy to resolve the problem.

1. What is the problem? _____

_____

_____

_____

2. List at least five ways to solve the problem.

a. _____

_____

b. _____

_____

c. _____

_____

d. _____

_____

e. _____

_____

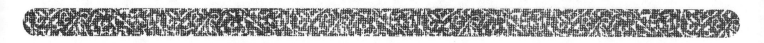

3. Choose the solution that you think would work best. Create a list of steps that would have to happen for this solution to work. _____

_____

_____

_____

_____

_____

_____

4. Plan what you are going to say to convince the two groups to try your solution.

_____

_____

_____

_____

_____

_____

_____

5. What can you say to both groups to convince them that you understand their points of view?_____

_____

_____

_____

_____

_____

6. Think about what the groups' objections are likely to be. Then write how you will answer these objections. _____

_____

_____

_____

_____

_____

_____

37 Writing to Inform
LESSON A Biography

What You'll LEARN
Writing a biography is more than just finding out when someone was born, what he or she did, and when he or she died. To write a good biography, you must make the story interesting to other people.

What You'll DO
First, choose someone whose life or work you admire. Then research that person's life. You can look in encyclopedias, books, videos, and magazine articles. You can even interview the person and others who know him or her. Take notes. You might want to look back at Lessons 8–12, Writing a Report, for more information about how to research and take notes.

What You'll WRITE
Write your biography on another sheet of paper. Before you write it, ask yourself these questions:

1. Do I know the basic facts about this person's life: spelling of the person's name, when he or she was born, where he or she was born and grew up, major events in his or her life, and date of death, if that applies?

2. Do I understand why this person is important? Why is he or she worthy of a biography? What impact has he or she had on the world?

3. Do I have some stories about his or her life that help the reader understand what he or she was like?

4. Do I have details about how he or she lived? What did the person look like? What did he or she like to do in for relaxation?

5. Do I have some quotations from the person that help explain the person's interests?

6. What is my purpose in writing the biography? Is it for a book-jacket cover, in which case it is intended to sell books? Is it for a newspaper obituary, in which case it should be an objective look at the person's life? Or is it written as part of a social studies book, in which case it should be informative and interesting?

7. How will I write the biography? You could choose to write the story of his or her life from birth to death. You could also start with the important things the subject accomplished and write mostly about those things. You could also focus on one important event in the person's life.

8. Make sure that your topic is narrow enough so that you are able to paint a clear picture of the person.

Writing Checklist

You may write a letter to apply for a job or a letter to a friend about a baseball game. No matter what you're writing, you can use this checklist to help you make sure that your ideas are heard and understood.

Prewriting. Before you pick up a pencil, you need to do some thinking about what you'll write and how you'll write. Answer these questions as you plan your writing:

❑ What is my purpose? Why am I writing? What message do I want to communicate?

❑ Who is my audience? Who will read my work? Answering this question will help you decide how you will write. If you are writing a letter to apply for a job, your letter will probably be formal. If it is a letter to a friend, your letter will have a friendlier tone.

❑ What kind of writing will I be doing? There are many different types of writing. These include letters, speeches, notes, and reports. You need to decide the kind of writing you'll be doing.

Research and Organizing. You need to know what you're writing about. In research papers, you may be doing formal research. In letters to persuade, you may need to gather facts. In this stage, you need to find information about your subject.

❑ Should I write an outline? For most types of writing, it makes sense to outline or even make a brief list of your main points. When you write your first draft, you can turn your outline into paragraphs.

Drafting. This is where you write the information you've gathered. In this stage, don't worry about grammar or punctuation. Put your ideas down, keeping these questions in mind:

❑ Do I have an introduction that tells the reader what I plan to say?

❑ Do I make my main points and use details to support them?

❑ Does my writing flow from one point to the next?

❑ Does my conclusion briefly restate the main point of the writing?

Revising. Here are questions to think about as you look over and revise your first draft:

❑ Have I checked my spelling, grammar, and punctuation?

❑ Have I read my writing to see if I can use better words or cut out unnecessary ones?

❑ Is my writing interesting? Would other people want to read it?

Preparing a Final Copy. After you have revised your writing, share it with a friend. Ask him or her the questions in the drafting and revising sections. Use the responses as a guide to creating your final draft. Then write or type a clean copy of your work.